# MAKING KINDLE WOOD OUT OF MY MOTHER'S THIGHS

Marthè Ndongala

Making Kindle Wood Out Of My Mother's Thighs by Marthè Ndongala
Published by Stain'd Arts
Denver, CO 80204

www.staindmagazine.com

© 2019 Stain'd Inc

All rights reserved. No portion of this book may be reproduced in any form without permission from the publisher, except as permitted by U.S. copyright law. For permissions contact:

help@staindmagazine.com

Cover by Delia LaJeunesse.

ISBN: 978-1-948850-05-6

Making Kindle Wood Out Of My Mother's Thighs is published by Stain'd Arts. To find out more about Stain'd peruse their work at Staindmagazine.com or contact info@staindmagazine.com

To read more of Marthè Ndongala's work, check out her website: themtnd.com/

# Table of Contents
:::

Mabelé — 3

Maì — 15

Mopepe — 29

Moto — 43

Ebendé — 57

Foreword

When I was a child in Africa, there was a woman that would walk up and down the market place in a white nighty dress. Her long black hair would be matted and covered in twigs. Her feet dirty and blackened from all the earth. Her eyes wild as she'd whisper incoherently to herself. She was beautiful. Or at least she once was. Her body was full in all of the places men's eyes lingered and her skin welcomed in the sun. Her beauty both wild and dirty was intoxicating and I remember a strange odor wafting from her. I know now she smelled of lust. The women in the streets would yell for her to leave, throwing buckets of water in her face. "Witch!" They'd scream foam falling from their mouths, sticks in their hands, violence in their eyes. "Whore! That's why you were cursed whore." My mother would steer my head away and tell me not to lock eyes with her. "She is cursed. She lives by the river alone because her family claimed that she was possessed. Someone cursed her." I remember watching her continue to walk, her hands covering her face as they pulled on her and beat her. She didn't run. All the hands and hate crashing upon her body, yet she still didn't run. Something deep inside me panicked, some voice in me rose and said "Run." My mother looked down at me and over to the woman. She watched me look. Although I was warned, I looked. Something about her ending and destruction called for me to witness and my small body was frozen like stone. My mother got up from where she was chatting with vendors and chased the people attacking the woman away. I watched as my mother yelled and cursed at them, saying something of their husbands' inability to keep their hands where they ate. The woman stopped and turned to my mother watching her steadily and my mother locked eyes with her. I gasped remembering her warning and ran over to her crying. "Why did you look Momma! Why did you look!" I clung to her skirt forcefully, my little hands grabbing as much of her as I could hold. She laughed and bent down until her eyes were level with mine. "What lives inside her, lives in us all. You cannot be scared of it, or it will consume you. " I couldn't understand what she meant at the time, but I was relieved she was safe. I turned my head and watched as the woman continued walking. She paused suddenly and slowly turned back, her eyes on me. They softened for a second taking in my childish face. My dark baby braids and my beautiful silk dress. I was small for my age. Always heard the coos and cries of women calling me a baby. I was soft and small, a doll on display. Part of me hated being treated like a child but I was one. I thought she was going to coo, to call out to my mother and comment on my delicate face and even smaller body, but suddenly her eyes darkened. Something began troubling her vision and I watched as her bruised face twisted in anguish and sorrow. She inhaled and suddenly screamed "Run!"

# Mabelé

I split
my lip
the first time
he
made
me smile.
Broke skin
and
promises of celibacy.
Paying
the price
of love
with blood
and flesh.
He kissed
my
unholy places.
He licked
away
iron
and
copper.
Freed me
from
one cage
and
used his
hands
to
carry me
into
another.
I held

my breath
counted
breathlessly
to five.
Tried not
to breathe
life
into this moment.
Tried not
to give
my life
to yet
another
man.
He peeled
the dead
skin
from my
lips
made my eyes
water
as I
was left with
nothing
but
raw flesh.
"There are
too many
layers
to you,"
he said.
"there must be
somewhere

in you
I can call home."
That night
I sat
on my lawn
and
pulled
at the grass
beneath me.
I buried
my fingers
into
the earth
and
began
eating
handful
after
handful
of
dirt.
I prayed
my
body would
take form
And the sorrow
would
swim up
and meet
my eyes.
I
refused
to let

this man
make
the
only home
I've ever
known
into
another
body

⋮

I carry
soil from my country in my pockets.
I hear
the laughter of children filter through my memories.
I dream
of thunderstorms that would silence a rainforest
and raindrops so heavy,
river ways would form in the middle of homes.
I see
the full moon smiling down upon us
God, embracing our darkness.
I count
my uncles as legion
feel their strong hands carry me
never allowing my feet
to kiss the ground.
I bounce
to the sounds of my grandmother singing hymns
in kikongo reverberates from the trees.
her brightly colored maputah
wrapping me tightly against her back.
I lose
myself to the rhythm of her heart beat
becoming one with mine
never knowing where she began and where I will end.
I take
bits of soil into my mouth each day
hoping one day
it will be enough to carry me home.

:::

I
Saw my mother in the kitchen.
Watched as she peeled onions
swallowing garlic cloves whole.
Her body
carried nutmeg and cumin.
Her chest
a swell of saffron and dill.

I
saw her
whispering
rapidly
causing the pots to boil
and the stew to burn.
She always said that
she was talking to angels
but
by the weight
of her face
and her shortness
of breath
something
made me
understand

for her
silence
was always
too heavy.

I
saw
my mother
turn
from me.
Her
dry voice
call me
over.
She
handed
me
her blade
and taught me
how
to slice through
tomatoes
without causing them
to bleed.

She
told me
my great
grandfather
taught her
how to
break flesh
but keep
what's necessary inside.
She said this
with her knife in hand

red juices running
down her arm
and splashing across her legs.
Her voice hitched
and her prayers
began
once more

I
saw my mother
turn her back
to leave
her body sagging
and whispers increasing.
"Who are you talking to Momma?"

:::

I caught myself
being more
burgundy than lilac
painting my borderlines
with vivid golds
smearing eyes
that once shadowed blue
with weighted browns
and watched as the
rivers crumbled
in my veins.
I was heavy with earth
and tried to
birth mountains
as my mothers before me.
collected sand
near my bed post
in wait
of a never ending storm.
the birds of prey
called with spirit song
in high notes.
shattered dreams
and window glass
in one
breath.
they caught me.
raising my hands
in surrender,
i chanted more
sullen songs
on lips unfamiliar with prayer
waiting for the dawn
to break and this
long night to be over.

:::

# Maì

Your soul calls
to me in the dead
of night. Even with all
of this darkness
you sound
like the voice of God.

:::

Let me
open
my veins
upon
parchment paper.
Speak
only
the truths
allotted
by silence.
Lick
my palms
and
place my hands
upon the gates
of the forbidden.
Bless the female form.
You are the first
and only sin
that man may justify.

:::

When my sister was 17
she smelled of nutmeg and wet oak.
Her hair grew past her shoulders and
covered her in thick black
darkness.
She never slept in her bed.
I remember nights finding her lying on the floor
her skinny body curled into a small ball.
She was dreaming.
Dreaming, of the days
when her body wasn't quite yet the world's.
My sister stopped going to church.
I saw her click her tongue at married uncles
and laugh until her tears turned into blood.
At night she'd comb my hair and say
"Your body is not a bridge.
Set yourself on fire when the time
comes."                   :::

White Lilies

A lily, like any flower, has its graces and vices. It invokes a strong tide of emotion deep within my belly I can't help but smile. This flower makes me think back to a period in my life where the color of the sky seemed to reflect the color of my dying love. During this time, every night seemed unilluminated. The moon and the stars hide themselves deep in the creases of heavens heart. So very far away from the gloom and doom that was him and I. As always there's a him to summon something inside of her, sometimes sweet, sometimes sinister. But truly, it all began when he brought home that vase of lilies. I remember walking into his room, tired and exhausted from a long day of work and another night spent clawing at each other's throats in the bed he had purchased for the purpose of making love. We seemed only capable of war. He was getting worse and our arguments began to tint the pure white walls of that small bedroom crimson red. But that afternoon, I was greeted with the white messengers instead of his normally erratic face. I swear those flowers were so chalky, even when they came to their end those unpigmented petals gleamed eerily. I know now those flowers consumed whatever grace there was left between us. I had placed my nose on their soft petals and realized they smelled like death. I don't know if he even knew, that those flowers symbolize a departing soul receiving innocence after leaving. There was an uneasy feeling festering deep inside my womb. I wasn't a woman that needed flowers for an apology, nor did I want them. I wanted my partner. I wanted the man I met who smelled of possibilities and patience. He was running out of options because the true issue seemed buried deep in the depths of his young soul. I thought about how stuck I felt, how everything was falling from the seams, including myself and thought about those damn lilies and paused. Maybe this was his way of preparing for my funeral. Well, one can only predict what happened after receiving such pleasantries. Our entire relationship eroded and turned both of us into dust. I said my goodbyes to the vase of dead lilies, the man that bought them, and walked into the sun for what felt like the first time in a very long time. Those flowers were the death of our relationship and the conductor of my freedom. Their gift was putting to rest something even I feared to bury. To this day, I hate lilies.

Wearing
creased
garments of white
Him and I
closed our legs
together
and watched
as rivers
run
from the
space
between us.
This
was the
night
of the
waning
moon.
A time
once used
to
banish
reverse
and
release
sorrow and pain.
You watched
as the stars
became inflamed
and slowly
began
their fall

from heaven.
Bringing
my hands
to the
sky
I
touched
the underbelly
of existence
felt the waters
break
free
from levies
and begin
to drown
us.
I
saw you
turn away.
Saw the
waters
run
 red
  and
   looked
  down
to see
the
blood
stained
between   us.
Tried to
hold you
as the darkness

seeped
in.
You
were the
only
light left
in
my existence.
I was taught to
fear the dark.
The blood
kept
running
and you
with it
leaving me
to
crash
between
waves
and
call for
my mother
as I
returned
to her
Womb.
There
was stillness
in these
waters
and
as I
lay here
held

by silence
and time
I
bent my back
praying
in old
tongues
hoping
to reverse
this spell
And
bring me
back
to the surface.
I fell
slowly
into darkness
hearing
the calls
and cries
of my
children
lost
long ago
at sea.
My white
gown
flowing freely
from my
body
wearing
the stains
of my humanity
as a

peace offering
and then
as an
act of war.
The stars
have now
reached
these waters
and my world
is engulfed
in
fire
and
metal.
I hear
as the waters
begin
to
recede
finding home
in
another
body.
I
am
woman
in my nakedness
but
I
still
hold you
in my form.

I
walk away
from the place
that buried me
and note
the call
of morning
take way.
It took me
less than
three
days
to rise
from
your grave.

:::

# Mopepe

Maybe you find solace in this loneliness
Remembering days when the stars would kiss your neck and the world was still yours. How quickly did we forget the moments of our infinity until we became bound by the smallest seconds of our past.

The body is water
nzóto iza mayi
le corps est de l'eau

but moments fall from us like sand in little hands.
Earth is no longer solid in your memory.
You were always falling.
But there was always a man
and a bed.
This kept you from drowning.
Yet beds aren't bodies and bodies aren't boats
so even in your room
where there was a man and a bed somehow
there was always
water and rain.
You were always drowning.

:::

I tread these bodies
in holy sacrament.
Let fire
and
Freedom
meet me
in deeper
waters.
I hear
the sound of
revelation calling.
These
are
the final days
where grace
is no more.
We are both
devils and demons
seeking
salvation
from other
fallen angels.
Hold me
dear God
for
the night
is long
and the
waters are
deep.
My body
is to be
bathed

but my body
is bloody
and swollen.
I smell
of the men
I've killed
and I
am ragged
in places
the world fed
from me.
Has darkness
ever
been given
such
a beautiful
ending?
White
lace
and
dark reds.
Black
eyed
and
brown skinned.
Let my
hands
reach
for the heavens
and let
the light
of the moon
fall

one
final
time.
These
are the
last
days
of men.

⋮

Felt heavy
but only
knowing hunger
devoured the fruits
of the season
knowing full
and
well
they were not
yet
ripe.
These moments
made memories
made mine
still bore
the stench
of the moon
and its lies.
There was nothing
left here
so
I was given everything.
Packed unripe fruit
and glass
then moved
away
from the place
that made
me a mother
and lover
before I
was anything
to myself.

It would be
Deceptive
to say
I
never
looked
back.
When
I did
I saw
what had to be
a mirage
of the man
I once
loved.
His body
tangled
and
broken
covered
in moss
and vines.
He was swallowed
by the
nothing
that was
everything.
As the void
took claim
of his body
I turned
myself
from him

Remembering
that nothing
in this world,
not even love
was mine.

      :::

We all
sat
around
the dying
flame.
My mother
her mother
and hers
before
her.
Their eyes
swollen shut
heads bowed
and their
hands
reaching
out
for warmth.
I
watched
as their
tears
ran
and collected
onto the
earth's
surface.
(She) The Earth
sprouted
small
dark
leaves
in center

of
their
tears.
Life
born
from
pain.
I
licked
my finger
and traced
small lines
from their
tears
to
the fire.
I
was
killing
Him.
(He) The Flame
of man
kept alive
by
the
bodies
of women
broken
betrayed
and
Never
given
burials.

I (God)
left
the circle
of my
lineage.
Broke
the cycle
of fire feeders
and embraced
the darkness
of those
who came
before them.
Heard
my mother
scream
as my
footsteps
grew further
away
but
never
did she
raise her head.

:::

Full
of flesh
and
shame
I
still seek
out
salvation
forgetting
that I
am
my own
savior

⋮

# Moto

Cursed fruit
tastes like
home front battles
in
dim lighted bedrooms
on
cold autumn nights.
It taste like,
first loves
fathering children
that aren't
your own
and listening
to a God
that tells you
to turn
the other
cheek.
He forgot
that your
left one
is marked
with
hand prints
but "nobody's
perfect" as your
husband would say.
Not even
god.
Cursed fruit
bleeds
the color

of
embryonic fluids
that cover
your newborn
because you have
nothing
to clean
him with.
It glows
the way
your baby's
paper thin
skin does
under white
fluorescent
lights.
After 20 hours
of labor
and a
close encounter
with death
you wait
for a taxi.
It looks
a bit like
mid drifts
and short skirts
that greet you
with "hellos"
during
Sunday service,
but the
only time

you've seen
their knees
on the
ground
is in front
of your
husband's throne.
I heard
it tastes
more like
swallowing sanctified
olive oil
hoping
to purge the
disease from
your body.
Hearing the word
"cancer"
on your
doctor's lips
is the
first time
in a long time
you heard
your husband
laugh
and you saw
that winning smile.
Oh, and how beautiful
was
that smile.
Sometimes though,
the skin looks

a little bit
like bruised
purple flesh
three broken ribs
teeth marks
on the right
side of your face
pieces
of glass stabbing
into your
bare feet
and dried
perspiration running
down your
open back.
I'm not sure
but it must
taste like tales
of long
work shifts
and untouched bodies.
The only heat
being felt
is from
God's promises
but for once
you prayed
for a man
to light
your skin
on fire.
Just once.
Would he

please
set you
ablaze.
Cursed fruit
is usually
fed to you
the moment
the hospitals
write 'girl'
on your
birth certificate
in the same
handwriting
they write 'woman'
in the morgue.
I think that's what it taste
like but soon, I'll know
for sure.

:::

fed from the roots.
became a god with no memory of being a woman.
became a man who knew nothing of love.
drank fluids from the living waters.
found myself in grandmothers womb.
found myself staring into mothers eyes.
laid with a man who spoke of stars.
sang with tears in my eyes.
sang with a heart that had to break to be opened.
ran away from my shadows.
used my soul to tell my story.
used my blood to break my ties.
laid my head at the base of the tree
then with a slow heavy breath returned to
the ones who first called me.

There are
no mirrors
in our
bedroom.
We stopped
being lovers
when your heart
told my body,
that I
was never yours.
When did we
stop speaking
the same
language?
At times it
seemed like Babylon
broke between us
and maybe,
just maybe,
even the sky
became jealous
of our love.
I was
too strong willed.
Held the world
on my back
and from the stars,
named
you Atlas.
But gave you
no compass.
You would
never find

a home
in me.
I couldn't
trust you
with my past
so
I limited
your time
in my future.
You have
no place here.
No one
to hold onto
and recite
empty lines
of promise.
Just me.
You never
look at me.
You face
the wall
every morning
and night,
continuing
to pretend
that you
are whole.
You laugh
and your teeth
thrash upon
your tongue,
nibbling at
what small

truths
remain.
There are
no mirrors
in our bedroom.
We see only
shadows dancing
across the wall
and place the world
in our
one way reality.
You no
longer
look at me.
You turn
your back
in the morning
and seek warmth
in another
woman's bed.
I hold my breath
between sunrise
and sunset,
trying not
to breathe
any more of
you in.
Say whispered
prayers of protection
knowing your eyes
only see me
in the dark.

Do you remember
that day?
I could
no longer stand
the sight
of my image
so
I salted
all the mirrors
and broke them
in two.
When asked
if I hated
what I saw,
I said yes.
Every time
I looked into
the mirror
all I saw was you.

:::

Our silence

There's this feeling, like early sunlight creeping into your bedroom and dancing on your skin. A feeling of dreaming something familiar and comforting but never knowing anyone's face or how the dream began. A feeling that calls you to sit and watch the leaves dance and the birds sing as if this is all there is to life, all that ever was. The distant laughter of children and the smell of flowers growing, mating, and blooming. This pervasive feeling that forces you to be still, to breathe slow, and to watch. Is it a feeling or an energy maybe, are they one in the same? This thing that calls to you in a group of people, in a crowded party, in a dimly lit house, and before the sun parts and ends another day. This heavy silence. It carries with it the songs our ears have forgotten but our hearts still know to listen for. This sound has carried me, has been the melody of my life's soundtrack, the silence that awakens me, and holds me in between breaths. Have we ever truly been alone? Surely not. For even in the loudest of moments, in the loudest places, the silence is with us.

# Ebendé

        reeked of many decaying dreams
        smelt the stench of molted memories
        and the smell of expired promises
        spoken on lips that knew the taste
        of the women who bore me.

I could not call to the waters
to take him from me for
they too knew

the hour of womanhood
was at hand.


what god would have me now...


that I smell of a man.


                :::

In the beginning
the   world
was
      darker
than
we   were.
I carried
halos  of  moons
around
my waist
and bathed
bodies
in pools
of hibiscus
      flowers.
Dared
to kiss
my
  own
    hands
and wash
my
feet
in juniper
wrapping yards
of hair
 around
  my
    sole.
I
was   pregnant
with
Hope

that year.
Bit
 too
  deeply
  into
him
and
filled
my body
with
the nectar
of
fruit
that
wasn't
quite
   yet
     ripe.
     There
was
a swell
in   my   belly
and a
sweetness
to
my
face.
Yet
the seed
of the fruit
and the flower
ripened
while

the source
was
unaware.
Lost
the
road
to
home.
Laid next to
faceless
 brown
  bodied
    women
whose shoulders
would shake
but
never
would
they
cry.
Lost
Hope
to
the
world.
Watched
as
her
mangled
body
was
placed in
a jar

and sold
as
freedom.
Became my mother.
Became me.
Found my face
in a
sea of
silent
tears.
Later,
I sold
the image
of
love
and
happiness
they
had sold me.
Became my father.
Became me.
Turned splinters
into
a crown
of thorns
held
my head
up to the sky
waiting
to be
called
home.

:::

We kissed in slow motion last night
You told me I was the first and only woman
to make your paper like body feel the weight of flesh.
You called to your god last night
You promised him in heavy breath that you'd give all
seconds in your existence to service if you could have this
moment, a small span of your eternity.
We danced in your cemetery that night
Every tombstone was inscribed with every date viability
was taken from you
You called me love that night
Said I embodied mercy, grace, and truth
Said all this with eyes closed, hands latched to my person
and never receiving my first name.
We drew blood last night
stained the walls with our violence and soaked the earth
with every sin that laid in all the mangled positions you
placed me. Called me little lamb and whispered prayers of
penitence over me.
You drew me into the wild last night
Said that I should feel at home here
I remember you bellowed into the old trees
"since your body refuses to be broken, I'll bend you into
millions of small pieces and I'll bury you in the bosom of
your mother. I promise."

:::

I'm not liked for my writing.
in truth, my words taste like
candle wax and lighter fluid
meant to be paired with the
matches buried deep
inside your belly.
I strike with syllables and song
like story telling turned sing along
that make you grow      feverish
restless
around your wooded campfire.
sweat
on  your  pink  lips
heat in places you were told
must
remain
cold.

I know.

I'm awful for this.
Cursed
words really.
they seem to
whisper
over your formless formalities
conjure resurrections
into your content composition.
the dead
aren't too keen on rising
pulling strings from silhouettes
and shadows.
always mocking,
"the illusion is no more, you are a real boy now."

I am not liked.
misinterpreted women
mean well
but often their words,
good and sincere
seem to cut
into thick skin,
each layer
placed by someone's somebody,
told by someone's somebody,
to lay down and
take both fire
and rain.
at certain angles,
broken bodies appear
to be standing upright.
men who look like you
point so freely at me.
"Eve"
they shout, "Eve!".
"mother"
they should say,
"oh mother."
they lick the earth
before they break it.
I see them nightly.
pull the tree tops apart
dig fingers into wet soil
looking at the sky
dead in the eyes
before they bring Her
to their mouths.
they taste
their dead mother
in the soil.

the decay
and iron
bring comfort
to their wretched souls.
one man panted
grunted as he dug up soil so red
the rivers began to scream
"that bitch brought me into this world," he shouted
"so it's only my right to show her out."
I wrote of this
so he disdains me too.
we are the same
the men who hate me
and I.
they,
the shadow.
I,
the alluded sun.
as I rise and fall,
their darkness
seems to
grow only bigger
heavier.
by the end
light
seems to swallow
the darkness whole.
only for it
to be reborn the next day.
I am not liked at all.

⁞

Tied

Love speaks a universal tongue. Both English, Native, and the heavy mixtures of those whose words were carried by the ocean and made love to foreign lands. Love is us. With our different backgrounds and mixed blood but blood will always take us back. Back, until we reach one man and one woman graced by an unknown infinite love. Love was between them, over them, under them, and inside of them. Love that had grown wild with time but understood purpose. Love, like a flower thorned and fragrant with silent beauty. Beauty, that causes all that was, to stop and take a long heavy breath. No words can convey this unknown infinite force, the catalysis of eternity. Love is our beginning. The questions of who, what, and when are echoed back with you, love, and now. We are fools in the way that only man can be, with our limitations in mind and our impossibilities as a disclaimer to what is our birthright. My son, my daughter do you truly believe you can pull God from a cell and create? It is not the cell that holds the power but the current used to conduct it into existence. What is love but divine alchemy? What is love if not the stone? What is love if not the eternal flame. Form, this container, is evident of the passion and patience of God's hand against the canvas of the Earth's surface. When two souls come into collision, a sense of knowing comes over them; like a shadowed visage across the face of time. We are meant to be broken. Each time we break the universe pours more of what we need into to us. So, break open. Break this heavy body filled with society's fears and failures wide open. Break the ideas of what should or should not be and allow yourself to simply be. Break open, and let the seeds of grace, joy, kindness, and of course love to bury itself inside you, bloom, and create life from has what has passed and died. This is you. Broken but beautiful. Bridled with passion, fire, song, and stars. Wild and untamed like God's first flower.

## About the Author:

Congolese born Marthè is a 24 year old Intuitive Counselor, Healer, Orator, and Creative residing in Denver Colorado. She is the child of a scientist and a housewife turned entrepreneur. Both are ordained in ministry, immigrants, and two worlds apart. She is those two worlds brought together. Using her work to describe her upbringing and her own truths she seeks to carry her ancestry, pain, joy, and vision from the light and into life's proverbial darkness. There it'll find room to transform and grow.

# About the Illustrator:

My name is Wemuht, an illustrator and story teller born in Houston and raised in Colorado. My journey began at a much later date than those before me but that hasn't stopped my desire to create. I vary in the type of work I do but I'm heavily geared towards digital illustration. However, there's a sweetness about traditional works. Watercolor has a specific uniqueness to it, it's uncontrollably free and I think that's what makes it so enjoyable. I started drawing when I was 11, but I was on and off until I was in college. My biggest inspiration comes from films directed and created by Hayao Miyazaki as well as game designer and art director, Tetsuya Nomura. I'm sure you've all heard of Howls Moving Castle and the Final Fantasy Series...yeah, those guys. Even in youth, I've spent my summer days watching anime and reading manga. Since then, I've become more drawn towards Japanese culture and it's been a great experience thus far! Even though I'm not where I want to be in this exact moment, my desire, persistence, and patience continue to propel me forward.

www.ingramcontent.com/pod-product-compliance
Lightning Source LLC
Chambersburg PA
CBHW041314110526
44591CB00022B/2906